NEIGHBORHOOD HELPERS

Electricians

BY CECILIA MINDEN

The Child's World

Content Adviser:
Eric David, Professor
of Electrical Technology,
Long Beach City College,
Long Beach, California

Published in the United States of America by The Child's World®
PO Box 326
Chanhassen, MN 55317-0326
800-599-READ
www.childsworld.com

Acknowledgements

The Child's World®: Mary Berendes, Publishing Director

Editorial Directions, Inc.: E. Russell Primm, Editorial Director; Katie Marsico, Managing Editor and Line Editor; Judith Shiffer, Assistant Editor; Caroline Wood, Editorial Assistant; Susan Hindman, Copy Editor; Wendy Mead, Proofreader; Mike Helenthal, Rory Mabin, and Caroline Wood, Fact Checkers; Tim Griffin/IndexServ, Indexer; Cian Loughlin O'Day, Photo Researcher; Linda S. Koutris, Photo Selector

The Design Lab: Kathleen Petelinsek, Design and Art Production

Photographs ©: Cover: left, right/frontispiece—Stockdisc.
Interior: 4—Photodisc/Getty Images; 5—RubberBall Productions; 7—Elva Tace/Alamy Images; 8-9—John Henley/Corbis; 10-11—Bill Bachmann/Alamy Images; 13, 19—T.J. Minden; 15, 16, 17—Stockdisc; 20-21—Sharon Stabley/Star Ledger/Corbis; 22-23—Tom Stewart/Corbis; 25—Ronald C. Saari; 26-27—Andy Sacks/Stone/Getty Images; 29—Roy McMahon/Corbis.

Library of Congress Cataloging-in-Publication Data

Minden, Cecilia.
  Electricians / by Cecilia Minden.
    p. cm. — (Neighborhood helpers)
  ISBN 1-59296-563-6 (library bound : alk. paper)
  1. Electric engineering—Vocational guidance—Juvenile literature. 2. Electricians—Job descriptions—Juvenile literature. I. Title. II. Series.
  TK159M56 2006
  621.319′24023—dc22   2005026216

TABLE OF CONTENTS

I Could Be an Electrician!. 6

Learn about This Neighborhood Helper! 8

Who Can Become an Electrician?. 10

Meet an Electrician!. 12

Where Can I Learn to Be an Electrician?. 14

What Does an Electrician Need to Do His Job? 16

Where Does an Electrician Work?. 18

Who Works with Electricians? 22

When Would an Electrician Need Superpowers? 24

I Want to Be an Electrician! .26

Why Don't You Try Being an Electrician?. 28

How to Learn More about Electricians 30

Index 32

Selena

Hello. My name is Selena. Many people live and work in my neighborhood. Each of them helps the neighborhood in different ways.

I thought of all the things I like to do. I like to take things apart to see how they work. I like to think of different ways of solving a problem.

How could I help my neighborhood when I grow up?

When Did This Job Start?

Houses and businesses began using electrical power in the late 1800s. Workers were needed to install electrical equipment.

I COULD BE AN ELECTRICIAN!

Electricians are good at working with their hands. They know how lots of different parts work together.

Best of all, electricians get to work in many different places and figure out interesting ways to solve problems.

Electricians know how wiring and many other parts all work together.

LEARN ABOUT THIS NEIGHBORHOOD HELPER!

The best way to learn is to ask questions. Words such as *who, what, where, when,* and *why* will help you learn about being an electrician.

Asking an electrician questions will help you learn more about his job.

Where Can I Learn More?

National Electrical
Contractors Association
3 Metro Center
Suite 1100
Bethesda, MD 20814

National Joint Apprenticeship
and Training Committee
National Training Center
301 Prince George's
  Boulevard, Suite D
Upper Marlboro, MD 20774

WHO CAN BECOME AN ELECTRICIAN?

Boys and girls who like science may want to become electricians. It is also important for electricians to be good at problem solving.

Electricians are an important part of the neighborhood. They keep people's lights and machinery working. Electricity powers everything from refrigerators to computers. Our world would be completely different without electricity!

Electricians make sure that electricity keeps flowing to homes and businesses.

How Can I Explore This Job?

Working with model trains will help you learn to use many of the tools electricians use. You can also talk to the custodian at your school. Discuss what kind of electrical work he or she does.

How Many Electricians Are There?

About 659,000 people work as electricians.

MEET AN ELECTRICIAN!

This is Manuel Olvera. Manuel is an electrician in Saint Louis, Missouri. He likes being an electrician, but he knows he has to be careful all the time. Electricity is important but can be very dangerous. When Manuel is not working as an electrician, he likes to spend time with his family.

Manuel knows it is important to be especially careful when working with electricity.

How Much School Will I Need?

People studying to be electricians must be at least eighteen years old and have a high school diploma. Electricians learn their job by working in an apprenticeship program. These programs last for three to five years. Electricians must also usually pass a test to get a license from the state where they live.

apprentices (uh-PREN-tiss-iz) students who learn a trade by working with people who are already skilled in that trade.

WHERE CAN I LEARN TO BE AN ELECTRICIAN?

Most people studying to be electricians learn what to do by working as **apprentices.** Students in an apprenticeship program often go to classes as part of training.

Electricians also need a license from the state where they live. But most electricians keep taking classes even after they get a license. Each state has rules electricians must follow when

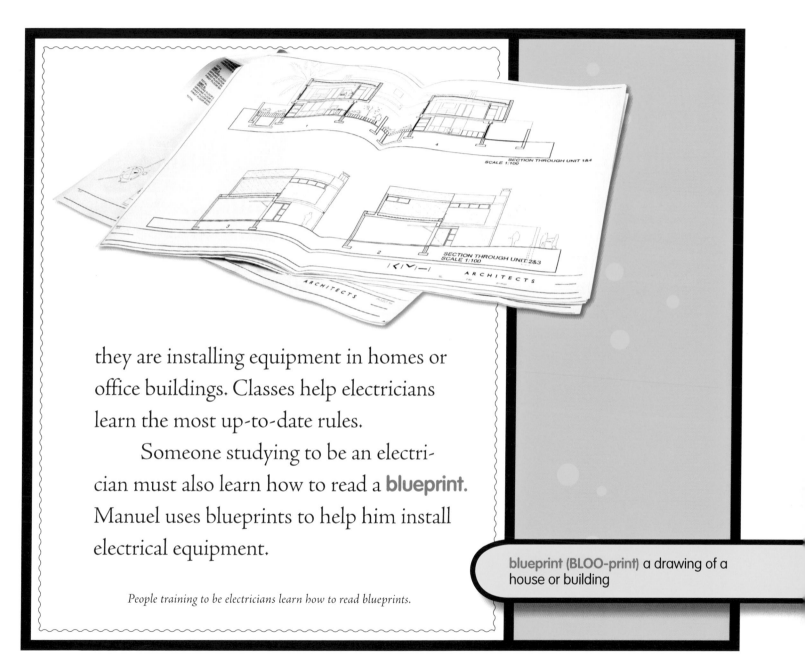

they are installing equipment in homes or office buildings. Classes help electricians learn the most up-to-date rules.

Someone studying to be an electrician must also learn how to read a **blueprint.** Manuel uses blueprints to help him install electrical equipment.

People training to be electricians learn how to read blueprints.

blueprint (BLOO-print) a drawing of a house or building

Blueprints

Hand tools

Ladders

Wire and cable

WHAT DOES AN ELECTRICIAN NEED TO DO HIS JOB?

Manuel uses many tools on his job. A few of these are screwdrivers, knives, pliers, and wire cutters. Electricians' tools have special insulation on them. This means they have a coating that prevents Manuel from getting hurt by the electricity.

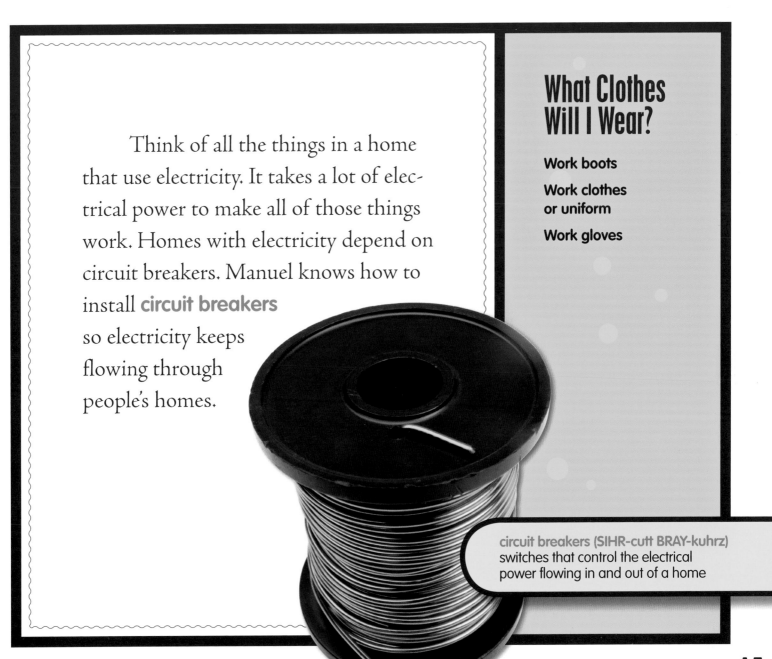

Think of all the things in a home that use electricity. It takes a lot of electrical power to make all of those things work. Homes with electricity depend on circuit breakers. Manuel knows how to install **circuit breakers** so electricity keeps flowing through people's homes.

What Clothes Will I Wear?

Work boots

Work clothes or uniform

Work gloves

circuit breakers (SIHR-cutt BRAY-kuhrz) switches that control the electrical power flowing in and out of a home

WHERE DOES AN ELECTRICIAN WORK?

Electricians work in many different places. Manuel works with electricity where people are building new businesses. These are called commercial buildings. He also works in new homes that are being built.

Other electricians work in maintenance. Has a big storm ever stopped the electricity in your neighborhood? A maintenance electrician probably fixed the power lines to bring back the electricity.

Manuel's job is different every day. He may be climbing ladders or working outside in bad weather.

Manuel sometimes puts wiring in new homes that are being built.

What's It Like Where I'll Work?

Electricians work both indoors and outdoors. Sometimes they work with circuit breakers inside a home. Other times they work outside and repair damaged power lines.

Sometimes Manuel has to work where it is dirty and hot. Other times he may have to work in a very small space. Manuel must always follow safety rules around electricity no matter what kind of job he is working on.

Electricians are also responsible for taking care of wiring in commercial buildings.

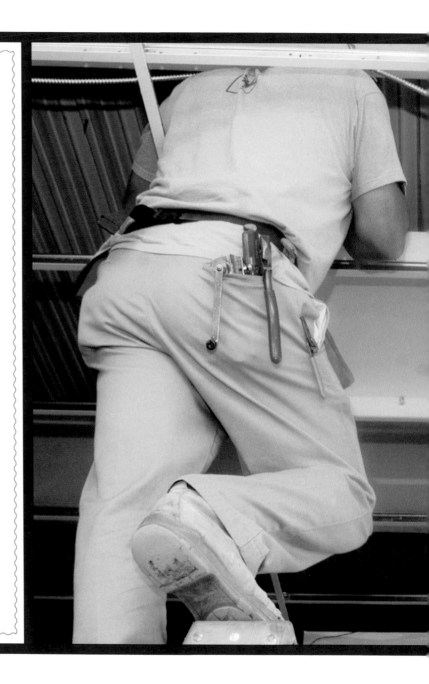

How Much Money Will I Make?

Most electricians make between $31,000 and $55,000 a year.

WHO WORKS WITH ELECTRICIANS?

Manuel works with carpenters, plumbers, and other electricians when he has a job at a new house. Apprentices also help Manuel and learn from him.

Electricians sometimes work with other craftspeople such as carpenters.

What Other Jobs Might I Like?

Aircraft mechanic

Drafter

Engineering technician

WHEN WOULD AN ELECTRICIAN NEED SUPERPOWERS?

The largest lightbulb in the world is in Menlo Park, New Jersey. It was built to honor the inventor of the lightbulb, Thomas Edison. This "super bulb" is 13 feet (4 meters) tall and weighs 8 tons. An electrician would have to make sure a lot of power was available to light up that bulb!

The world's largest lightbulb lights up the night sky over Menlo Park.

How Might My Job Change?

Some electricians start their own businesses. Others gain experience in someone else's company. They may eventually be in charge of other electricians at that company.

I WANT TO BE AN ELECTRICIAN!

I think being an electrician would be a great way to be a neighborhood helper. Someday I may be the one to install electricity in your home!

Are you interested in working with electricity? One day you might help light up people's homes!

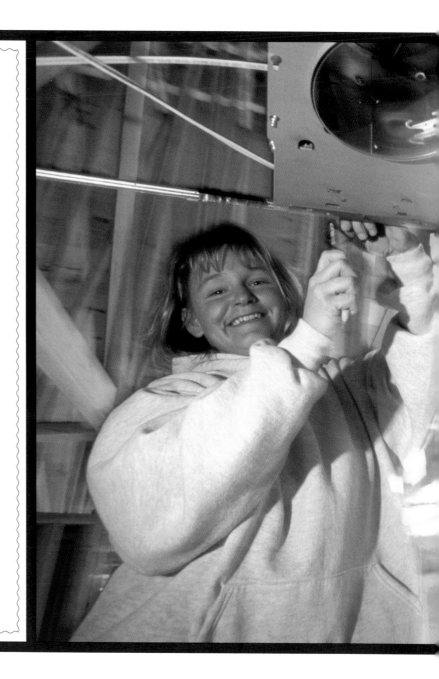

Is This Job Growing?

The need for electricians will grow faster than other jobs.

Benjamin Franklin is famous for his experiments with electricity in the 1700s.

static electricity (STA-tik i-lek-TRIH-suh-tee) electricity created by rubbing two objects against each other

WHY DON'T YOU TRY BEING AN ELECTRICIAN?

Do you think you would like to be an electrician? You can start by learning about different types of electricity. One type is **static electricity.** Have you ever walked across a carpet, touched a metal object, and then felt a shock? This is caused by static electricity.

Blow up a balloon. Try to get the balloon to stick to a wall. It will fall off.

Now rub the balloon on the top of your head and try again. The balloon will probably stick to the wall this time. Static electricity causes this to happen.

What a hairdo! Static electricity can make your hair stand straight up.

HOW TO LEARN MORE ABOUT ELECTRICIANS

BOOKS

Cast, C. Vance, and Sue Wilkinson (illustrator). *Where Does Electricity Come From?* Hauppauge, N.Y.: Barron's, 1992.

Lytle, Elizabeth Stewart. *Careers As an Electrician.* New York: Rosen Publishing Group, 1993.

Overcamp, David. *Electrician.* Danbury, Conn.: Children's Press, 2003.

Thomas, Mark. *A Day with an Electrician.* Danbury, Conn.: Children's Press, 2001.

WEB SITES

Visit our home page for lots of links about electricians:
http://www.childsworld.com/links

Note to Parents, Teachers, and Librarians:

We routinely check our Web links to make sure they're safe, active sites—so encourage your readers to check them out!

ABOUT THE AUTHOR:

Dr. Cecilia Minden is a university professor and reading specialist with classroom and administrative experience in grades K–12. She is the author of many books for early readers. Cecilia and her husband Dave Cupp live in North Carolina. She earned her PhD in reading education from the University of Virginia.

INDEX

aircraft mechanics, 23
apprenticeship programs, 14, 22

blueprints, 15, 16
boots, 17
businesses, 6, 18, 24

carpenters, 6, 22
circuit breakers, 17, 19
classes, 14, 15
clothes, 17
commercial buildings, 18
custodians, 11

drafters, 23

Edison, Thomas, 24
electrical equipment, 6, 10, 15
electricity, 6, 10, 12, 16, 17, 18, 20, 26, 28, 29
engineering technicians, 23

Franklin, Benjamin, 28

gloves, 17

homes, 6, 10, 15, 17, 18, 19, 22, 26

insulation, 16

knives, 16

ladders, 16, 18
licenses, 14
lights, 10, 24

maintenance electricians, 18
model trains, 11
money, 21

National Electrical Contractors Association, 9
National Joint Apprenticeship Training Committee, 9
need, 27

Olvera, Manuel, 12, 15, 16, 17, 18, 20, 22

pliers, 16
plumbers, 22
power lines, 18, 19
problem solving, 5, 6, 10

questions, 8

rules, 14–15, 20

schools, 14
science, 10
screwdrivers, 16
static electricity, 28–29
"super bulb," 24

tests, 14
tools, 11, 16
training, 14

uniforms, 17

wire cutters, 16